AXOLOTLS

by Jaclyn Jaycox

PEBBLE
a capstone imprint

Published by Pebble, an imprint of Capstone
1710 Roe Crest Drive, North Mankato, Minnesota 56003
capstonepub.com

Library of Congress Cataloging-in-Publication Data
Names: Jaycox, Jaclyn, 1983- author.
Title: Axolotls / by Jaclyn Jaycox.
Description: North Mankato, Minnesota : Pebble, [2023] | Series: Animals | Includes bibliographical references and index. | Audience: Ages 5-8 | Audience: Grades K-1 | Summary: "Axolotls have gills, but they are not fish. They are amphibians! Unlike other amphibians, though, axolotls spend their whole lives in the water. With easy text and colorful photos, young readers will have fun finding out more about these unique creatures"— Provided by publisher.
Identifiers: LCCN 2022000657 (print) | LCCN 2022000658 (ebook) | ISBN 9781666342741 (hardcover) | ISBN 9781666342789 (paperback) | ISBN 9781666342826 (pdf) | ISBN 9781666342901 (kindle edition)
Subjects: LCSH: Axolotls—Juvenile literature.
Classification: LCC QL668.C23 J39 2023 (print) | LCC QL668.C23 (ebook) | DDC 597.8/58—dc23/eng/20220202
LC record available at https://lccn.loc.gov/2022000657
LC ebook record available at https://lccn.loc.gov/2022000658

Image Credits

Alamy: blickwinkel, 21, Roberto Nistri, 22; Capstone Press, 6; Getty Images: aureapterus, Cover, kwiktor, 9; Newscom: Zuma Press/Carlos Tischler, 14; Shutterstock: Anney_Lier, 11, Arm001, 13, 28, Charlotte Bleijenberg, 18, Erni, 7, Guillermo Guerau Serra, 17, Henner Danke, 25, Jay Ondreicka, 10, Lapis2380, 1, 5, 8, 12, 19, Marchgami, 26, Santiago Castillo Chomel, 27

Editorial Credits

Editor: Abby Huff; Designer: Dina Her; Media Researchers: Jo Miller and Pam Mitsakos; Production Specialist: Tori Abraham

All internet sites appearing in back matter were available and accurate when this book was sent to press.

Table of Contents

Words in **bold** are in the glossary.

Amazing Axolotls

An odd animal lives deep in the water. It looks like a lizard. But it has feathery-looking **gills**. What could it be? It's an axolotl! Its name is said *AKS-uh-lot-uhl.*

Axolotls are a type of salamander. They are **amphibians**. Usually, young amphibians live in the water. Then they go on land as adults. But axolotls spend their whole lives in the water!

Where in the World

Axolotls are found naturally in only one place on Earth. They live in Lake Xochimilco. This is a freshwater lake. It's in Mexico City, Mexico.

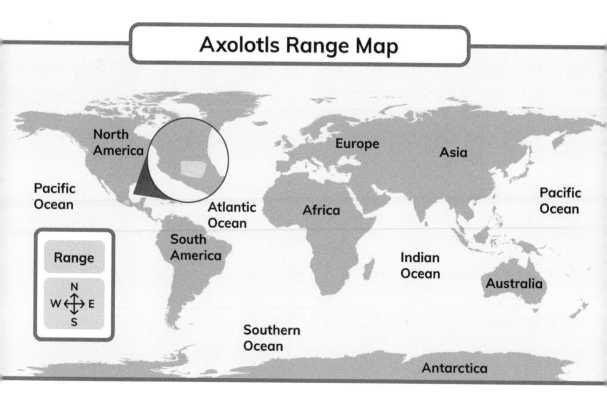

Axolotls Range Map

North America

Europe

Asia

Pacific Ocean

Pacific Ocean

Atlantic Ocean

Africa

South America

Range

Indian Ocean

N
W E
S

Australia

Southern Ocean

Antarctica

Pet axolotls live in fish tanks.

Only a small number of these animals live in the wild. But there are many around the world raised by humans. Axolotls are found in zoos and research labs. People also keep them as pets.

Axolotls spend most of their time in deep water. Adults don't often swim. Instead, they walk on the ground at the bottom of the water. Some people even call them Mexican walking fish.

During the day, axolotls hide. This keeps them safe from **predators**. Axolotls dig into mud. They hide in plants. At night, they hunt for food.

Axolotl Bodies

Axolotls blend in with muddy water. They are often black or greenish-brown. But they can change color. They can get lighter or darker. It helps them hide in plants and rocks.

White and pink are popular colors for pets.

Some axolotls are white or pink.

But this is not common in the wild.

Many light-colored ones are pets.

Axolotls grow to about 9 to 18 inches (23 to 46 centimeters) long. They have long tails. A fin grows down their backs. Webbed feet help them push through the water.

These animals have big, flat heads. Feathery gills stick out on both sides. They don't have eyelids. They sleep with their eyes open!

Axolotls have big mouths. When their mouths are closed, the corners bend up. It looks like they are smiling!

Axolotls being kept by scientists

Axolotls have a special skill. They can regrow body parts. A predator might bite off an axolotl's leg. But a new leg will grow. An axolotl can also grow a new spine, jaw, and lungs. It can even regrow its heart and parts of its brain!

Scientists are studying these animals. They are learning about how axolotls regrow parts. They hope it will help people with missing limbs someday.

On the Menu

The day is over. Night is here. An axolotl stands quiet and still. It senses a fish nearby. It opens its mouth and sucks in. *Slurp!* The **prey** is pulled into the axolotl's mouth. Yum!

Axolotls eat worms and small fish. They eat tadpoles and insects too. They are not picky. If the food fits in their mouths, they will likely eat it.

An axolotl eats an insect.

Axolotls will hunt by keeping still.

Axolotls hunt in a few ways. They will swim to the surface. They catch bugs here. But often they stay on the bottom of the water. They wait for food to swim by. Axolotls can't see well. They sense movement instead.

An axolotl catches prey with its mouth. It sucks up food like a vacuum. It has very small teeth that aren't good for chewing. So it swallows its food whole.

Life of an Axolotl

Axolotls live alone in the wild. But males and females come together to **mate**. Mating season is usually from March to June.

Females lay eggs on rocks and plants. They can lay 300 to 1,000 eggs at a time. The eggs hatch about two weeks later. The babies are called **larvae**. They are smaller than a dime!

Eggs almost ready to hatch

A young axolotl with only its front legs fully grown

Axolotls don't take care of their young. Each larva is on its own. They start hunting for food a few hours after they hatch.

The larva has gills, a head, and a tail. Its skin is so thin, you can see its **organs**. After a few weeks, its front legs grow in. Its skin darkens. A couple weeks later, it gets back legs.

Many amphibians go through **metamorphosis**. Young start as larvae. Then they grow lungs. They lose their gills. They are ready for life on land. But axolotls are different.

Axolotls grow lungs. But they rarely use them. They stay in the water. So they keep their gills and tails. Young axolotls look like small adults.

In about six months to a year, axolotls are ready to mate. They are now adults. They usually live 10 to 15 years.

Axolotls spend all their lives in the water.

Dangers to Axolotls

Large fish like tilapia and carp eat axolotls. Birds such as storks and herons will snatch them too. But their biggest danger is humans.

heron

Lake Xochimilco is the only place axolotls live in the wild, but the water is getting dirty.

Cities near the axolotls' lake are getting bigger. The lake is becoming **polluted**. Trash, plastic, and other waste spill into the water. Some areas are too dirty for animals to live.

Axolotls are in danger of dying out in the wild. Their numbers are going down. Less than 1,000 wild ones are left in Mexico.

People are working to help. Groups are trying to clean up the lake. They want to keep these amazing animals around for many years to come.

Fast Facts

Name: axolotl

Habitat: freshwater lakes

Where in the World: Lake Xochimilco in Mexico City, Mexico

Food: worms, small fish, tadpoles, insects

Predators: tilapia, carp, storks, herons, humans

Life Span: 10 to 15 years

Glossary

amphibian (am-FIH-bee-uhn)—a cold-blooded animal with a backbone; it usually lives in the water when it's young and on land as an adult

gill (GIL)—a body part used to breathe underwater

larva (LAR-vuh)—a young animal at the stage of its life cycle between an egg and an adult

mate (MEYT)—to join with another to produce young

metamorphosis (met-uh-MOR-fuh-sis)—the series of changes from a young form into a very different adult form

organ (OR-guhn)—a body part that does a certain job

polluted (puh-LOO-ted)—dirty and harmful to living things

predator (PREH-duh-tur)—an animal that hunts other animals for food

prey (PRAY)—an animal hunted by another animal for food

Read More

Bassier, Emma. *Axolotls*. Minneapolis: Pop!, 2020.

Kenney, Karen Latchana. *Axolotls*. Mankato, MN: Amicus Ink, 2018.

Potts, Nikki. *It's Still Alive!: Magical Animals That Regrow Parts*. North Mankato, MN: Capstone Press, 2018.

Internet Sites

Active Wild: Axolotl Facts For Kids
activewild.com/axolotl-facts-for-kids/

Animal Fact Guide: Axolotl
animalfactguide.com/animal-facts/axolotl/

National Geographic Kids: Mexican Axolotl
kids.nationalgeographic.com/animals/amphibians/
facts/mexican-axolotl

Index

About the Author

Jaclyn Jaycox is a children's book author and editor. She lives in southern Minnesota with her husband, two kids, and a spunky goldendoodle.